ELIXIR III
BE CAREFUL WHAT YOU WISH FOR
BY JACK MARINCHEK

Contents

Chapter 1

All hell is breaking loose at Starlight Pharmaceutical in Ruskin, Florida. Ruskin is a small town on Florida's West Coast, approximately 30 miles south of Tampa. Something has gone terribly wrong with Starlight Pharmaceutical's youth restoration drug known as Elixir. 28 people have been reported to have recently died because of taking Elixir. People at Starlight Pharmaceutical Corporation are scrambling to find out what is causing this catastrophe.

Specifically, Carlos Bolivar, the driving force behind the creation of Starlight 's Elixir and Carlos's chemist and partner, Frank Rafferty, the Australian born chemist who discovered Elixir,' are working night and day to find a fix for their star youth restoration product, Elixir.

Until recently, everything was going beautifully regarding the sale and distribution of Elixir. Sales have been going thru the roof. People in America simply can't get enough of the youth restoration drug called Elixir.

And rightfully so. Hell bells Mary Lou, what person nearing the ripe old years of 50 wouldn't want a youth restoring drug like Elixir? Elixir is almost guaranteed to get you looking and feeling like you were when you were 21 years old. I kid you not! Just go to the beach sometime and catch a glimpse at the guys and gals wearing those slim bathing suits showing enough body so that there is little left to the imagination. You think you're looking at a 21 year old. I swear to God. It turns out a lot of these guys and gals have been on this planet for 50 plus some years. Yeah...believe it!

Not only that, but you should get a look see at what is happening in the bedrooms of Mr. and Mrs. Middle America. I mean what you have going on at nights for these youth restored Americans, thanks to Elixir, is some red hot smoking passion between the sheets. Sex has suddenly taking a number one priority for many marriages that not so long ago found sexual activity a cumbersome obligation. Not anymore. Couples and partners, thanks to Elixir, are smoking hot between the sheets. Amen brothers and sisters and hallelujah.

Speaking of hot romantic passion, let me refer you to the evening happenings of Carlos Bolivar and his longtime girlfriend Danielle Simpson. These two lovers have been in a steady relationship for over five years now. Danielle has been instrumental in helping Carlos and Frank getting the youth restoration drug Elixir off the ground. Carlos admits he is one very lucky "old guy". Danielle happens to have a body of a much younger woman. She definitely has the sex appetite of a much younger woman. Both Danielle and Carlos are personally very strong advocates of Elixir. We can take a quick peek into Danielle's bedroom last Thursday evening:

"Oh fuck me Carlos. Please baby, rub my pussy while you stick your cock in my ass….O-O-O-H-H-H Carlos Baby. It feels so good. Please Lover….don't stop. Do it! Do it!" moaned Danielle Simpson as her ass gyrated with heat.

Carlos jerked and pumped his hard as steel cock, penetrating Danielle deeply as he fingered her pussy until her wet cum oozed onto his fingers. Then Carlos shot his cum all the way into Danielle's ass, rolled over and proceeded to get up from the bed. "Danielle, you are the greatest sex goddess on planet Earth."

"Hip hip hooray for Elixir. America's answer to Paradise on Earth", yelled Danielle.

"You got that right sugar pie. Elixir keeps my dick hard like a pussy warrior should be."

It started two weeks ago. Reports were coming in about people dying for seemingly little to know reason. Then, it was discovered that all of these people were Elixir users. One thing led to another, and finally the culprit of these unexplained deaths turned out to be the world famous youth restoration drug called Elixir. The scary part about this Elixir business is that nobody seems to have a clue of why Elixir is killing people and comparatively speaking, only a few people. Distribution of Elixir pills is in the millions.

Chapter 2

Carlos and Frank are staying up nights, going without sleep, making a desperate effort to find the cause of Elixir's seemingly malfunction which has purportedly killed several people. Unfortunately, nobody knows what the reason is for this problem.

These sudden 28 deaths caused by Elixir have both Carlos and Frank climbing the wall. On the other hand, if you were to pick two people who would handle a crisis which exists with this Elixir business, it would be Carlos Bolivar and Frank Rafferty.

Carlos is no stranger to crisis management. He personally led his platoon of Marines out of an ambushed firefight while he was a lieutenant platoon leader during his tour in the Vietnam War. As a matter of fact, he received a bronze star for valor for his heroic action during that specific action. Not to, mention Carlos's seemingly propensity for creating his own good fortune.

After Carlos's tour with the Marines, Carlos got involved with martial arts and ended up creating his own martial art called Psy kwon do. Psy kwon do is a combination of Tae Kwon Do, Aikido, and mental psychokinesis, a mind over matter thing. While applying the moves of Tae Kwon Do and Aikido the participant visually imagines the force and movement of these martial arts which gives a lethal force and intensity that cannot be denied. Carlos's Psy Kwon Do became very popular which allowed him to create a national franchise of Psy kwon Do martial art schools. The result of this franchise business left Carlos and very wealthy man.

Frank Rafferty, on the other hand, has tasted success down under in his own right. Frank has enjoyed success as the lead chemist for a very well known Pharmacy in Sydney, Australia. After Frank's retirement, Frank continued his love for chemical research on his own in an independent capacity. Frank through trial and error discovered the chemical properties which eventually led to the discovery of the famous youth restoration drug known as Elixir. Again, Carlos used his magic to bring Elixir to a reality.

Danielle Simpson is actually the third ingredient that is responsible for the creation of Elixir, counting Carlos Bolivar and Frank Rafferty as ingredient number one and two. It was Danielle Simpson who actually set the financial wheels rolling for Elixir. She contacted her deceased husband, Donald Simpson's partner, David Cassidy of Cassidy and Rothstein, a venture capital firm in San Francisco for venture money for Elixir's market opening in the United States. Both Carlos and Frank have very strong loyalty ties to Danielle, in addition, to Carlos having Danielle as his confidant and girlfriend.

"Frank, are you sure manufacturing is following the same formula when we began with Elixir?"

"Carlos, no question about it. I have personally checked the records. Nothing has changed. However, after checking around, I am afraid things are worse than I anticipated."

"What are you talking about?"

"Carlos, you won't believe this but Elixir is actually doing the best job it could considering how I programmed it chemically....Please, hear me out. I have discovered that Elixir, that is, its chemical compounds, are doing exactly what that are programmed for. They are causing the genes that cause aging to wither away and give way to youth restoration. Whereby people are reverting to their genes that where dominant when they were 21 years old...this process is what we call youth restoration. But, in some rare cases, people who have the Calendar Gene, and not many do, the youth restoration gene overrides to a certain extent the maturity gene."

"Frank, what the hell does that mean?"

"Carlos it means in those very rare cases which I just described, where the maturity gene is arrested in the inhibition mode, these people continue to get younger and younger. Eventually, their internal organs become like embryos in the womb and people die from organ immaturity.

"My God, what can we do about that?"

"Carlos, fortunately, there are not many people that are receptive to advanced age regression. But there are enough to stop Elixir in its tracks. Somehow, we have to find and antidote for this problem. There must be someone in this world who can help us solve this problem. I mean, I don't want to sound cold hearted, but General Motors doesn't stop building automobiles because people are killing themselves because they are driving too fast. There must be an answer to this problem!"

Chapter 3

One afternoon, sitting at his desk and feeling very despondent, Carlos received a call from a woman named Mary O'Hare. This woman, apparently has contacted Carlos about Elixir. She requested an appointment to discuss with him the tragedy which Elixir is causing. Mary indicated to Carlos that she believed she could help Carlos with his Elixir problem considering her background in gene therapy. Carlos was made aware of Ms. O'Hare last week by a newspaper column where she commented on the apparent malfunctions of Elixir. She added some authority to the news piece because she is a highly accredited gene therapist and researcher. Carlos thanked O'Hare for calling and made an appointment to see her the following day at his office.

At the meeting with O'Hare the following day, Mary O'Hare informed Carlos and Frank that she thought she could help with the Elixir problem. Well at this stage of the game, Carlos and Frank felt they had nothing to lose.

"Yeah, go ahead Mary. Do your thing," encouraged Frank.

To Carlos's surprise, Mary was not at all what he expected. She was very pretty. He thought she'd be a real bookish kind of woman. But, she wasn't at all. Frank also was very impressed with this woman.

"Fellows, here's what I would like to do for you regarding Elixir. As you know, my expertise is gene engineering. What I'd like to do is take a sample of Elixir to my office and have my staff check out its chemical composition.

"Believe me, if there is anything funny going on with Elixir, I'll find it. You have had Elixir on the market for 18 months, right?"

"Yes."

"OK. And I assume up until recent, you have had no problems or reported deaths relating to Elixir?"

"Correct."

"Ok gentlemen. If you will provide me with a specimen of Elixir. Then, I will be on my way."

"Excellent Mary. So nice meeting with you," said Carlos.

Mary received a specimen of Elixir and then picked up her briefcase and exited Starlight Pharmaceutical.

Approximately one week later, Carlos received a call from Ms. O'Hare informing him that her research on Elixir was finished and that she'd be over to his office tomorrow afternoon.

At 2pm Friday, in Carlos's office, Mary O'Hare presented her findings to Carlos and Frank.

"Fellows, it's like this: Nada, no problems with Elixir. Clean as a whistle. My staff couldn't find anything that was abnormal for your youth restoration drug.

"Now, there is one possibility that could explain the sudden death of some of your Elixir users."

Carlos and Frank looked at each other knowingly. "And, what might that be Mary?" inquired Frank.

"You fellows know my specialty is gene engineering. So I am on top of most issues like we have with Elixir. I mean, like I pull down some hefty consulting fees with some of this country's biggest pharmaceutical firms, just doing what I am doing for you, that is troubleshooting.

" Ok Mary. So….?"

"Right. Here is my theory why your Elixir is killing some people. In some cases, people who have the yz chromosome in their immune system, are subject to increased cellular age regression. It's an extreme age regression process that turns mature people into infants and eventual death.

"Please don't misunderstand me. The extreme age regression I am referring to is confined to the subject's internal organs. It's the internal organs of these unfortunate people with the flawed yz chromosome that becomes total regressed to the point that the organs are in an embryo state and a subsequent death occurs."

Frank leaned forward in his chair, "Mary, I must tell you, last week I informed Carlos here that the maturity gene in Elixir, when it was arrested in the inhibition mode, caused extreme age regression and killed people. Which of course verifies what you just told us. Elixir is killing people who have this flawed yz chromosome.

Mary nodded.

"So Mary, what can we do about this problem?" asked Carlos.

"Great question Carlos. If you will permit me." Mary got up from her chair and walked over to the chalk board. "Gentlemen, here's what

I propose: We take the nucleus of Elixir's active cell which arrests the regressive age gene and add a very small amount of protein matter to it. This should check the flawed yz chromosome that is killing your Elixir users. Then your problem with Elixir should be solved and there will be no more fatalities for the people who do have the flowed yz chromosome."

Carlos and Frank looked at each other. "Mary, if you can do what you just proposed, stop Elixir from killing people, I guarantee you that you will have two very grateful guys. Believe me, you will never have to work another day in your life," said Carlos.

"Thanks Carlos. Now let me get on with my work." Mary turned towards Carlos's office door and walked out.

Chapter 4

Three weeks later Mary O'Hare came trotting into Starlight Pharmaceutical's office. She was almost at the main receptionist's desk when Carlos whispered into the receptionist's ear, "Sherri, this is Mary O'Hare coming to you. Get used to her because from here on, we all will be seeing a lot of Ms. O'Hare."

"Well thanks for the vote of confidence Carlos. I hope you are right on that score," commented Ms. O'Hare.

Carlos knew he was right. He could feel it in his bones. This Mary is going to save his ass from total disaster regarding Elixir's propensity to kill people.

Carlos took Mary's hand and led her into his office. They both sat down. "So Mary, what do you have for me?"

"It's done Carlos. I added the protein factor to Elixir's cellular nucleus. All of our follow up tests prove conclusively that Elixir no longer has the capacity to hurt people with the defective yz chromosome."

Both Carlos and Frank were elated. "Mary, you just added ten more years to our lives."

Frank Rafferty and Mary O'Hare became very good friends soon after Mary's official association with Starlight Pharmaceutical. Mary was put in charge of the chemical research department at Starlight. Frank continued to act as an advisor to Mary's department.

It didn't take long before Frank and Mary were working together in unison on a very hush hush project activity dealing with embryo engineering and gene manipulation. The project became officially known as Embryo Sym. Specifically Embryo Syms purpose was to create a human baby without the use of an actual female carrier. In another words, what you have in theory, is an embryo egg created by a male and female donor, which is harvested and nurtured in a factory like environment, whose sole purpose is to create baby boys and girls.

Embryo Sym purported to eventually produce Designer Babies that could have a predominance of characteristics that where designated by the adopted parents. In another words, if a couple wished to have an athletic child who possessed the characteristics of a super tennis player with blue eyes and blond hair, Embryo Sym could deliver the goods. That's right ladies and gentlemen, Designer babies will now be a reality in America if Embryo Sym becomes a reality. You want a Special baby, just call up Starlight Pharmaceutical. They will make one for you. Oh, and the delivery date is still 9 months!

The Society for Traditional Values recently got wind of Starlight's new product, Designer Babies and Embryo Sym. The Society is not happy about this at all. In fact, James Cullen is furious. He feels like he was betrayed by Carlos Bolivar and Frank Rafferty. After all, it was James Cullen and his Society for Traditional Values that put up the money for the initial development of Elixir when The Society provided the venture capital for Starlight's Elixir during some crucial stages.

Carlos picked up his Iphone to take a call from James Cullen, the president of The Society for Traditional Values. The Society is actually a lobbying firm focused on helping the insurance industry. It was James Cullen who persuaded the top echelon of the insurance industry to embrace Starlight's youth restoration drug, Elixir. James primary motivation for backing Elixir had to do with the fact that Carlos and

Frank were instrumental in introducing Elixir to James's son, Matthew of was suffering from Multiple Sclerosis. Elixir cured Matthew of the disease. Naturally James Cullen felt indebted to Carlos and Frank. This is why the Society ended up raising venture capital for Elixir; thus, helping Elixir get off the ground.

Carlos gets on the telephone with James Cullen, "Hey James, what's happening?"

"Carlos we need to meet. How about the Fountain Inn tomorrow for lunch?"

"Sure. OK Carlos. See you then," replied James Cullen.

Carlos was walking into the entrance of the Fountain Inn in Ruskin and he suddenly felt a light tap on his left shoulder. He turned around, and sure enough, standing there was his luncheon partner, James Cullen.

"James, nice seeing you. What a coincidence?"

Carlos turned around, "Yeah, right. Let' go in and get something to eat."

The two men picked a table with a great view of the Gulf of Mexico. They sat down and began ordering lunch as the waiter took their orders.

"So, James, what did you want to see me about?"

"Carlos, we have known each other a long time. I am grateful for what you and Frank did for my son Matthew, with your Elixir product.

Matthew has been totally cures from his MS disease. I have you all to thank for that.

What concerns me now is this EmbroyoSym business."

"How so James?"

"I am getting hammered by my associates at The Society because of this new product you guys at Starlight Pharmaceutical are trying to bring out. I am talking about this Embryo Sym business. The manufactured process of artificially producing human beings. You know, these factory style designer babies you want to sell on the open market!"

"Look James, we are a long way from taking Embryo Sym to the market. You know, we need FDA approval, and the whole ball of wax. I feel positive a lot of your objections and concerns will be answered in a positive manner in the not too distant future. We have a new executive on board at Starlight that is running the show for Embryo Sym. A woman named Mary O'Hare. She is a gene therapist by training. She has a PhD degree in chemistry."

"Carlos, my concerns with Embryo Sym deal with the subject of artificial production of human beings. We, rather myself and most of the members of The Society for Traditional Values are standing back in disgust with the idea that potentially men and women will no longer be having babies in the conventional way. You know what I am talking about, the normal process of cohabitation between and man and woman. Hell Carlos, everyone is going to want a Designer Baby...their own customized, made to order, baby."

"Easy does it James. I know where you are coming from. In fact, initially, when I first heard about this program, Embryo Sym, I in all honesty, expressed the same concerns you are presenting to me now.

"Here's what I think we should do James. Next week, you and I will have lunch here again with Mary O'Hare. She's my executive who is running the show regarding Embryo Sym. You can ask her any questions you want. How does that sound?"

"Carlos, it's a deal."

James put his hand in his inside breast pocket of his shirt and pulled out a newspaper clipping. "Carlos, here is something you might want to dwell on a little bit."

James handed over a copy of the news print from yesterday's Wall Street Journal: "Starlight Pharmaceutical has been hit with another lawsuit regarding Elixir, the youth restoration drug, which is blamed for the wrongful deaths of 28 people who were users of Elixir."

Carlos put the Wall Street Journal article down on the table. "Yeah. So now James you can see my life isn't exactly all roses. For your information James, we have corrected that problem with Elixir. See you next week?"

James nodded and both men got up from the table and walked out of the restaurant.

Chapter 5

Two weeks later we fine a big pow wow at the headquarters of Starlight Pharmaceutical.

Everybody is all dressed up. In the executive conference room of Starlight Pharmaceutical there are a whole bunch of new faces. Apparently a group from the Society of Traditional Values, led by James Cullen are present.

Carlos, Frank, and Mary O'Hare are at the head of the conference room table.

"Meeting come to order," bellowed Carlos Bolivar.

"Ladies and gentlemen, the order of business today is to debate whether Starlight Pharmaceutical should continue pursing to bring to market its latest experimental drug which is purported to artificially create life. We know this process as giving human beings the ability to have Designer Babies. Starlight's product name for this project is called Embryo Sym.

"First we will have the discussion and then vote on this question. Frank or Mary, do either of you wish to comment?"

Frank nodded in the negative. Mary smiled and stood up, "Ladies and Gentlemen, I realize I am new to Starlight Pharmaceutical, but since I am in charge of the Embryo Sym project, I feel it is obligatory of me to volunteer some information at this meeting about Embryo Sym."

In response, a few positive nods were thrown in from the attendees.

"Thank you. As most of you know, Embryo Sym is very close to being ready to go to market. All of our testing and research on this life creating drug is complete. Basically, when Starlight gets FDA approval, we will begin production of this drug.

"Exactly what need will Embryo Sym feel? I will be specific. Before Embryo Sym was created couples that wanted children were subject to their own heredity genes. In another words, newborns were the product of their parent's genes, namely, heredity.

"Not anymore folks. Thanks to Embryo Sym, parents can have their very own designer baby. You want a super jock with blond hair and blue eyes? You got it with Embryo Sym. Am I right Frank?"

Frank nodded in agreement.

"So, that's the story of Embryo Sym. Anybody got questions?"

James Cullen from The Society of Traditional Values raised his hand, "May I"

"Sure Mr. Cullen. Please go ahead," acknowledged Mary.

"I guess we the people of the United States having finally arrived to the era of Big Brother in government. One of the last bastions of individualism, the Family Unit and childbirth are going by the wayside. Now we have approaching our society, if Embryo Sym becomes a reality, factory made human beings. We are taking God and mother nature out of the equation of childbirth. What's next? Government sponsored marriage and cohabitation? I mean give me a break people. How far are you willing to go with this business. Hell, a couple years ago, you folks at Starlight gave Americans Elixir.

"Yes, Elixir, a youth restoration drug, like no other. Now we can't tell the difference between the 21 year olds and 70 year olds. Everybody looks like they are 21 years old. People not only look young but they are for all practical purposes, they are young in both mental, emotional and physical capacity.

"I'm not inferring that Elixir is a bad thing. No sir. My own son, Matthew Cullen, had MS. Thanks to Frank Rafferty and Carlos Bolivar, and their Elixir product, my Matthew is now cured of MS. Elixir cured him of that dreadful disease. Thanks to Elixir, nobody is sick or dying anymore. At least not to the degree they were before Elixir. I am just afraid that we are going to have more government in our lives here in the United States. This factor to me is very worrisome."

Carlos Bolivar stood up, "James, I appreciate your concern about Big Brother, that is big government interfering in the private lives of Americans. But, hey James, it's Starlight Pharmaceutical that's the game player here, not Uncle Same. Are you forgetting that?"

"Carlos, I hear you. I know where you are coming from. But, I guarantee you, it will just be a matter of time and we will have big government getting involved with baby planning and your Embryo Sym product."

"Sure. So you say James. We will deal with that when it happens."

Ok ladies and gentlemen. Now that we have had our discussion, I am putting forth the motion that Embryo Sym be approved by this panel of shareholders. All in favor, raise your hands. And all againt, raise your hands. Ladies and gentlemen, the yeses have it. Embryo Sym will be submitted to the FDA tomorrow. Mary O'Hare, you are the Starlight Pharmaceutical executive in charge. Get to it and good luck."

"Thank you Carlos and Frank for your vote of confidence. Ladies and gentlemen I am sure you won't be disappointed," replied Mary O'Hare.

And with that ending the shareholders meeting at Starlight Pharmaceutical was ended.

Most Americans are enjoying the benefits of Elixir, the youth restoration drug which Starlight Pharmaceutical manufactures. Why wouldn't they? Your average middle aged man and woman is walking around looking and acting like a 21 year old. They are enjoying life like no other American generation has ever been so fortunate to experience.

Job security is great now. Dick and Jane have the experience of a 50 year old combined with the youth and vitality of a 21 year old. Employers know they have tremendous assets in these rehabilitated, youth restored, Elixir men and women.

Life expectancy is great. Nobody is getting sick or dying anymore. Not in today's Elixir dominated society. Most of the nursing homes, funeral homes and hospitals are dying or going out of business. James Cullen's Society for Traditional Values lobbying for the insurance industry is having a very tough time of it. People aren't buying life or health insurance anymore. Hardly anyone is getting sick or dying. Life is good from that standpoint.

There are some storm clouds on horizon. I am talking about problems brewing from the federal government. The current ruling administration in Washington D.C. is beginning to focus on the problems of the population growth in the United States caused by Elixir because very few people are dying. In another words, America's natural resources simply can't handle the current population growth rate. Will this lead to a national governmental population growth management by deciding who can and can't have babies? Time will tell!

The subject of who and who can't have children is becoming a concern by the government. This problem is highlighted by the ever growing presence of a drug supposedly being developed by Starlight Pharmaceutical; namely, Embryo Sym.

Mary O'Hare has a definite opinion about future products that will come to market for Starlight Pharmaceutical. She has been working quite fervently on a hush hush project dealing with the proposal of humans having the capacity to use the full capacity of their brains.

She initially got this idea of brain acceleration from Carlos Bolivar. Carlos has mastered his mind to the point that he actually uses all of his mind. Specifically he has learned to managed his subconscious which approximates 90% of the human mind. Carlos discovered these mind accelerant strategies were discovered and developed by Carlos during his foray into his development of his psy kwon do, which is a composite of maximizing mind and physical martial art.

The future for Carlos Bolivar, Frank Rafferty and Mary O'Hare is both challenging and surprising.

THE END